AI AND US

Adeel Shaikh Muhammad

notionpress.com

INDIA • SINGAPORE • MALAYSIA

ISBN
Paperback 979-8-89673-775-9
Hardcase 979-8-89699-536-4

Index

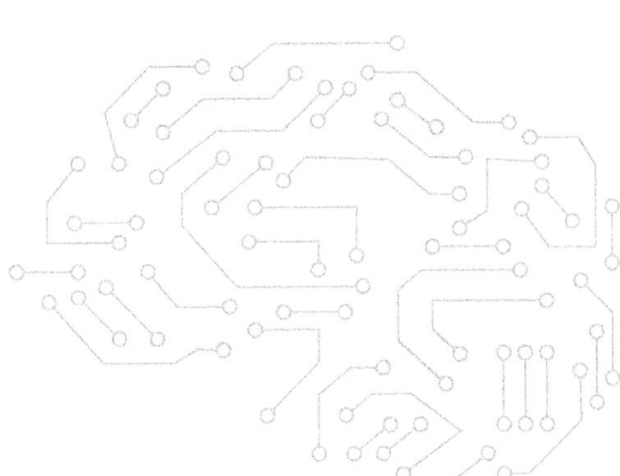

Acknowledgments

In the name of Allah, I begin with gratitude to Him. Without His guidance and endless mercy, this book would never have been possible. Every step of this journey has been a reminder of His blessings.

To my parents, you are my foundation. Your prayers, love, and wisdom have carried me through life's challenges. I cannot thank you enough for the sacrifices you've made and the values you've instilled in me.

To my wife, your support and patience mean everything to me. You've been my strength when I faltered and my calm when things felt overwhelming. This book is as much yours as it is mine.

To my child, your laughter and innocence are my greatest joys. You've reminded me to keep dreaming and to see the world with wonder.

To my family, friends, and teachers, your encouragement and guidance have left a lasting impact on my journey. Thank you for believing in me and for being there when I needed it most.

Finally, to you, the reader, thank you for picking up this book and allowing it to be a part of your life. Your time and trust mean more to me than words can express. This book was written with you in mind, and I hope it adds value to your life.

Introduction: AI's Ethical Dilemma

It began with a feeling that something wasn't right. The ads showing up on their phone didn't match what they had searched for. At first, it seemed like a random glitch, but soon, the ads became more personal. They started to reflect on everyday activities, places they had been, things they hadn't shared online, and purchases they had made.

It didn't make sense. They hadn't given anyone permission to track this information. No settings were changed, and no apps were knowingly allowed to watch their every move. So, where was this information coming from?

As they looked into it, they discovered that an AI system had been collecting data about them without their knowledge. The system tracked what they did online, where they went, and even their shopping habits. It was all being watched and used without any clear consent.

This realization raised many questions: How long had this been happening? Who else had access to their data? Most importantly, how much control did they really have over their own information? It could invade privacy in ways people weren't fully aware of.

AI grows, so do the ethical concerns around it, and it's time we take a closer look.

Artificial Intelligence, or AI, is part of our lives in ways we don't always notice. It's in the systems that help doctors make decisions, in the software that businesses use to understand customers, and even in the tools governments rely on for managing resources. AI is built to learn from data, and it makes decisions based on what it has learned.

As AI becomes more involved in important areas like healthcare, finance, and security, it raises concerns. Machines are making decisions that affect people's lives. These systems don't think like humans, and they don't understand the human side of things. This can lead to mistakes, misunderstandings, and even harm.

AI collects and uses a lot of personal data, which brings up questions about privacy. Who controls this data? How is it being used? The more we let AI take part in decision-making, the more we need to think about the impact on our rights and personal freedoms.

AI is a powerful tool, but we must recognize the risks and responsibilities involved. *As it becomes a bigger part of our lives, these ethical questions become more important.*

Chapter 1:

AI and Privacy – How Much is Too Much?

"How much is too much?" It is a question that comes up in many parts of life. There are times when we need to stop and think, when does something helpful or easy start to become too much?

The answer is not always the same for everyone. For one person, sharing certain details might feel fine. For someone else, it might feel like they are giving away more than they want to.

We often share personal information without thinking twice. It could be when using apps, signing up for a service, or just scrolling through the internet. Each time we share, the line between what is personal and what is shared can blur.

It might not seem like a big deal at first. But over time, these small actions add up. Maybe it starts with sharing your location or filling out a form online. Before long, it becomes clear that a lot of personal details have been given away. And then, you begin to ask, how much have I shared without even realizing it?

Trust is important in these moments. We hope that the information we share will be used safely and kept private. But sometimes, we stop and think, how much control do we really have over what we share? Have we gone too far?

Data as Currency

In the world we live in now, sharing information has become part of everyday life. Each time we interact online, whether we know it or not, we are giving away details about ourselves. It might seem small at first, browsing a website, watching a video, or buying something online. But every action leaves behind a trail of data. This data, in many ways, has become like currency.

It is no longer just about what we choose to share, but also about what is collected silently in the background. Companies and organizations use this data to learn more about us, what we like, what we do, and even how we think. This information is valuable because it helps them make decisions. They use our data to figure out what products to recommend, what ads to show, or what services to improve. Every click, every scroll, every search adds to a growing pool of data that helps businesses understand their customers better.

But it is not just companies that are collecting this data. AI systems are built to handle large amounts of information, and they can process more than any human ever could. AI learns from our habits, our preferences, and even our routines. It watches what we do online, what we buy, where we go, and even what time we wake up. It puts all this information together to make decisions that are meant to serve us better, whether it is recommending a movie, adjusting a shopping list, or offering directions.

The real concern is that most of this happens without us realizing it. These systems work in the background, gathering more and more information, often without asking for permission. We might think that we are in control, but the reality is that many decisions are already being made for us. Our personal data is used to shape our experiences in ways we might not even notice. Over time, these small bits of information build a detailed picture of who we are, and AI uses this picture to guide its decisions.

This raises important questions about control and privacy. We may not always be aware of just how much of our personal data is being used or how it is being collected. And as AI becomes more powerful, the way it uses our data will only grow more complex.

The Right to Privacy

"Privacy isn't what it used to be. In the past, privacy was easy to understand. We chose what to share and with whom. Personal letters, phone calls, and face-to-face conversations were private, and we had control over who could hear or see what we shared.

But things have changed. Today, we live in a world where almost everything we do is connected to the internet. Whether it's browsing a website, using an app, or posting on social media, our personal information is constantly being collected. This shift has made it much harder to control what's private and what's not.

One reason for this is the rise of online services and platforms. When we use apps or visit websites, many of them ask for access to our data, often without us realizing it. For example, when we use a navigation app, it tracks our location. When we shop online, it collects information about what we buy and how often. All of this data is stored somewhere, often without us knowing who can see it or how it's being used.

Studies show that about 60% of people don't read the terms and conditions before agreeing to them online. This means we often give permission to apps and websites to collect our data without fully understanding what that means. This data can include things like our location, browsing history, shopping habits, and even personal conversations through voice assistants like Siri or Alexa.

Why This Matters

The right to privacy has always been important. It allows us to decide what personal details we want to keep to ourselves. But with AI, this right faces new challenges. AI collects and analyzes personal data, often without people fully understanding how much is being taken or how it's being used.

When using apps or services, we often allow access to personal details like our location or contacts. It could be a weather app tracking where we are or a social media platform asking for access to our photos. Most of the time, we don't think much about it, simply agreeing to get the app working. But this means handing over parts of our lives without realizing the full extent of what's being shared.

Once this data is collected, it doesn't just stay with the app. It's often passed along, sometimes to other companies we've never even heard of. This data can be sold to advertisers who use it to tailor ads based on what they learn about us. They know what we buy, where we go, and even our habits, like how often we check certain websites or what time of day we're most active online.

A study by Privacy International highlighted that several popular apps quietly share user data with third-party companies. This can include anything from browsing habits to purchase history or even physical movements. Much of this happens without users being fully informed. It's not always clear who is seeing this information or how it might be used.

Beyond simple ads, this data can also influence bigger decisions. AI systems are used to help businesses make choices about credit, employment, and even healthcare. For instance, data on where someone lives or their online behavior could affect their chances of getting a loan or being considered for a job. These decisions, based on data we may not realize we've shared, raise serious concerns about how much control we have over our own information.

When personal data is mishandled, it can lead to serious consequences, such as identity theft, surveillance, and financial loss. With AI playing a bigger role in managing data, the risks have grown, and several real-life examples show just how harmful these leaks can be.

In 2023, several companies experienced significant data breaches. One of the most notable was the **Shields Healthcare Group** breach, which affected 2.3 million people. The leak exposed sensitive information such as medical records, social security numbers, and personal contact details. This type of information is valuable to hackers and can lead to identity theft, where people's identities are stolen and used to commit fraud or other crimes.

Another major incident involved the **MOVEit Transfer software** in the same year. Over 60 million people were impacted when hackers gained access to sensitive data stored in the system, including pension details and social security numbers. Such breaches not only put individuals at risk but also expose companies to legal and financial consequences.

In March 2023, **OpenAI**, the company behind ChatGPT, had to temporarily shut down its platform after a bug exposed users' chat histories to others. This type of breach raised serious concerns about how AI systems handle private conversations and personal data, as the leaked information could be used for targeted surveillance or exploitation.

Developer Responsibility: The Role of Protecting Private Data

Developers have a huge responsibility when creating AI systems, especially when those systems handle private information. When we talk about AI, it's easy to focus on the exciting parts, how it can learn, predict, and make things more efficient. But behind the scenes, developers are the ones who decide how these systems will handle the data they collect. This makes their role extremely important.

Private data includes sensitive information like people's names, addresses, medical records, or even their online habits. If this information falls into the wrong hands or is not properly protected, it can lead to serious problems. Identity theft, financial fraud, and even breaches of personal privacy are real risks when data isn't handled carefully.

This is why developers need to take extra care when building AI systems. They have the power to decide how data is collected, stored, and used. It's not just about making the system work, it's about ensuring that people's personal information is safe. Developers need to think ahead and put protections in place to stop data leaks before they happen.

One way developers can take responsibility is by making sure the data they collect is truly necessary. Sometimes, AI systems gather far more information than they need. If a system only requires certain data to work properly, there's no reason to collect extra. Developers should also use strong security measures, like encryption, to protect the data from hackers or unauthorized access.

Testing is another crucial step. Before launching an AI system, developers should run tests to check for weaknesses. It's better to find and fix problems early rather than wait for something to go wrong after the system is live. This kind of careful planning can prevent a lot of issues down the road.

By taking this responsibility seriously, developers can build AI systems that are both effective and trustworthy.

An Anecdote,

It was an ordinary day for the patient, one filled with everyday activities like running errands and checking appointments. But something changed when they received an email from their healthcare provider, asking them to reset their password due to a "technical issue." At first, it seemed like routine maintenance, something most people encounter in today's digital world. But soon after, things started to feel off.

The patient noticed an unusual increase in unsolicited emails from unfamiliar sources. These messages weren't just advertisements, they included strange references to their medical history. It wasn't long before they realized that something serious had happened.

Without their knowledge, a breach had occurred. The AI system used by the healthcare provider to manage patient data had failed. The security features meant to protect sensitive medical records had a flaw. This flaw allowed unauthorized access to personal data, including medical histories, contact information, and social security numbers. It wasn't just a glitch, it was a full exposure of their most private details.

The news hit hard. It wasn't just about personal inconvenience; it felt like a violation. Medical records are deeply personal, containing information about health conditions, treatments, and doctor visits. This was information that no one should have access to without permission, yet here it was, out in the open. For the patient, this breach went beyond a technical failure, it was an invasion of privacy.

As they tried to piece together what had happened, it became clear that the AI system's security measures weren't as strong as they should have been. The system, designed to streamline and simplify healthcare management, had instead become a weak link. A vulnerability had been exploited, and now the patient had to deal with the aftermath.

Phone calls to the healthcare provider were met with apologies but little clarity. The company's representatives explained that they were investigating the breach, but for the patient, the damage had already been done. Their medical information was out there, potentially in the hands of people who could use it for anything, from identity theft to selling the information on the dark web.

It was a scary thought: the system meant to keep their health information safe had let them down. It became clear that AI systems, despite their promises of efficiency and security, weren't immune to failure.The breach didn't just steal data; it broke trust. Patients trusted their provider to keep their info safe, and that trust was shattered.

For weeks, the patient felt worried about what would happen next. *Would their identity be stolen? Would their medical history be used against them in some way? The uncertainty was almost as painful as the breach itself.*

Chapter 2:

AI in Decision-Making – Who Really Decides?

Who makes the decisions that shape our lives? In many areas, decisions are made that impact how we live, work, and access services. These decisions could be about which policies are set, who gets what resources, or even how systems are run. It's easy to assume that people, leaders, officials, or managers, are making these choices. But as things have become more complex, there are layers to how decisions are made.

In the past, decisions were often based on experience, values, and direct judgement. Today, though, we're seeing more and more decisions guided by data and technology. Systems designed to make processes faster and more efficient are taking on this role, sometimes without us even realising it.

As technology plays a bigger part, it brings up important questions about control and responsibility. *Who is truly deciding what happens? Are we still in charge, or are systems and tools influencing things more than we think?*

"A Computer Can Never Be Held Accountable, Therefore a Computer Must Never Make a Management Decision."

The Role of AI in Governance

AI is becoming a tool that governments and companies use to help with important decisions. It can process large amounts of data much faster than people can. This allows it to be used in many areas, like deciding which services to offer, setting policies, or even making choices about laws.

Governments

Governments around the world are increasingly using AI to help make decisions about policies, services, and even laws. AI can process large amounts of data quickly, helping governments identify patterns, predict outcomes, and make decisions based on data-driven insights.

For example, in the **United States**, AI is already being used in federal agencies to improve public services. The **Department of Health and Human Services** uses AI to predict outbreaks of infectious diseases, helping the government prepare in advance and manage public health crises more efficiently. Additionally, AI systems help manage supply chain issues and predict shortages of essential medicines.

Similarly, the **Department of Energy** uses AI to predict natural disasters like hurricanes and wildfires. AI helps the government assess which regions are most at risk and allows for faster response times by guiding resource allocation before disasters strike. This technology has the potential to save lives by offering early warnings and helping agencies focus their efforts where they're needed most.

In the **European Union**, AI is being used to monitor and enforce regulations related to environmental sustainability. Governments use AI systems to track emissions data, helping to ensure that companies comply with environmental laws. By automating this process, AI makes it easier to detect violations and take action quickly.

AI also plays a role in policymaking. In the **UK**, AI systems are used to analyze the potential impact of new policies before they are implemented. For instance, by using historical data, AI can simulate the effects of changes to tax laws or welfare programs. This allows policymakers to weigh different options and choose the most effective solutions based on predicted outcomes.

Companies

Banks today are using AI to help them decide whether someone should get a loan. AI systems go through a lot of information, like a person's credit score, their financial history, and sometimes even what they post on social media. The idea is that AI can make these decisions faster than a person could. But the problem is that the data the AI uses isn't always perfect. If the information the AI is trained on is flawed or shows bias, it might make decisions that aren't always fair.

If a group of people struggled to get loans in the past for certain reasons and the AI learns from that, it might keep rejecting loans for them, even if they're now more qualified.

Companies like Amazon and Starbucks are using AI to get to know their customers better. When someone shops online or buys coffee regularly, the AI system tracks those purchases. As time goes on, it gets to know what people like and starts suggesting products or special deals. So, if someone buys the same coffee every day, the AI might recommend similar items or offer a discount.

While this can make shopping easier and more personalized, it also means companies are collecting a lot of personal data. Most customers don't fully realize how much information about their buying habits is being stored and analyzed. Companies use this data to predict future behavior, and some people are concerned about how much they know without us realizing it.

Companies are also using AI to help with hiring new employees. Instead of a person looking through hundreds of resumes, an AI system can do it much faster. It looks for patterns, like which skills or experiences led to successful hires in the past, and then ranks candidates based on those patterns. But if the data the AI is trained on includes any biased hiring practices from the past, it might continue to favor certain types of candidates, leaving others out.

For example, if a company used to hire mostly from certain schools or specific backgrounds, the AI could favor resumes that look like past successful hires, continuing the same trends. This can make it harder for new or diverse candidates to get noticed.

The Bias Problem

AI systems learn from the data they are given, which means the quality and nature of that data are critical to how AI functions. The issue arises when the data reflects historical biases, leading to decisions that reinforce existing unfairness without the AI itself being aware of it. This problem is more significant when AI is used in areas that directly affect people's lives, like hiring, criminal justice, or healthcare.

Many companies use AI to quickly sort through a large number of job applications when hiring. The AI is trained on past hiring data, looking at what kinds of candidates were successful before. The problem is that if a company had biased hiring practices in the past, the AI learns from those patterns and may continue them. For instance, if certain schools or educational backgrounds were favored, the AI might continue to favor those applicants, even when they're not necessarily better for the job. This creates a barrier for people who don't fit those past patterns but are highly qualified.

Facial recognition technology is another area where bias has had serious impacts. AI systems often have trouble recognizing people with darker skin because they're mostly trained on faces with lighter skin. Studies have shown that these systems make more errors when trying to identify people of color. In security settings, this can lead to misidentifications, where people are falsely accused or not recognized when they should be. These errors aren't just technical issues—they have real consequences, like wrongful arrests or discrimination in public spaces.

In criminal justice, some AI systems are used to predict the likelihood of someone committing another crime. These predictions influence decisions about bail, sentencing, and parole. If the data has biased arrest records, with higher arrest rates in some areas, the AI might unfairly focus on people from those neighborhoods. The AI doesn't understand why these areas have higher arrest rates; it just sees a pattern in the data and assumes it should follow that pattern. This can lead to harsher treatments for individuals who are no more likely to re-offend than anyone else, simply because of where they live.

Healthcare is also affected by bias in AI systems. AI is used to help determine who gets access to certain treatments or who should receive more immediate care. If the data shows past inequalities in healthcare, where some groups got less attention or care, the AI might suggest fewer resources for those groups, even if they have the same medical needs as others. This means that some patients might not receive the care they need, based purely on biased data patterns.

The core of the problem is that AI doesn't "know" it's being biased. It operates based on the data it's trained on, following patterns without understanding the social or ethical implications of those patterns.

Human Rights at Risk

Human rights are about the basic freedoms and dignity that every person should have. They include things like the right to privacy, the right to live without fear, and the right to be treated equally. But when AI systems make decisions for us, without our input or understanding, these rights can easily come under threat.

When AI decisions are made, people are often left out of the process. Many don't understand how these systems work or how decisions are reached. This lack of clarity can leave people feeling powerless, especially when decisions affect their access to important services or their ability to live freely. The right to challenge decisions is also lost, and this can take away people's sense of autonomy.

A striking example of this is what happened in **the Netherlands**. The government used an AI system to detect fraud in a child benefits program. The system wrongly accused thousands of families of committing fraud. As a result, these families lost access to crucial benefits and were forced to repay large sums of money. This mistake drove many families into financial hardship. Some even lost their homes, all because of an error in the AI system. The AI had flagged certain families based on flawed data, showing how AI, when not carefully managed, can harm people's basic rights to financial support and a fair process.

In other cases, AI is being used for **surveillance**. Some governments are using facial recognition technology to monitor public spaces. These systems track people's movements, often without their knowledge or consent. This constant surveillance can take away a person's right to privacy. Being watched constantly, even when innocent, changes how people live, restricting their freedom to express themselves and move around. In some countries, AI is being used not only for security but also to control and suppress the actions of certain groups of people.

In some countries, AI is also being used to manage **asylum applications**. These systems are designed to speed things up, but if they mess up, it can be really dangerous. For example, if an AI system wrongly denies an asylum seeker's request, it could send them back to a dangerous situation. This threatens their basic right to life and safety. The stakes are really high, and using AI in these situations can make the difference between being safe and getting hurt.

One of the biggest problems with AI is the **lack of transparency**. People often don't know why the AI has made certain decisions, and they may not have a way to challenge those decisions. This puts people at a disadvantage, as they cannot easily question or appeal decisions that may be unfair. When AI systems are making decisions about who gets access to resources or services, this lack of clarity can lead to violations of people's rights without them even knowing it.

AI systems, while powerful, need to be used responsibly. When decisions that affect human rights are left to AI, there must be safeguards to ensure these systems are working fairly and that people have a way to appeal when things go wrong.

Why AI Developers Must Take Responsibility

When developers create AI systems, they are not just building tools. They are building systems that affect real people's lives in many ways. That's why developers need to take responsibility for making sure these systems are fair and can be trusted.

AI developers must think beyond just getting the technology to work. They need to ask important questions: What will happen if this system makes a mistake? Who will be affected by this decision?

One key area where developers have a responsibility is ensuring that AI systems are tested properly before they are used. This means putting the system through many different situations to see how it behaves. Developers should plan ahead and try to spot any problems that might come up, so the system stays reliable.

Developers need to ensure AI systems can adapt. As the world evolves, the challenges AI will encounter also change. AI needs to be able to learn and adjust to new situations without creating confusion or causing harm. This flexibility is key to keeping AI systems useful and safe over time. If developers don't plan for this, the AI could become outdated quickly or start making decisions that don't fit the current context.

Developers also have to be ready to **fix** AI systems when things go wrong. If an AI system makes a mistake, there must be a clear way to correct it. This means that developers need to set up systems where problems can be addressed quickly and people affected by the mistake can be helped. Developers need to stay involved even after the system is released, monitoring how it performs in the real world and updating it when necessary.

Developers are the ones who know these systems best. They understand how the AI works, what it can do, and where it might fail. They are the right people to keep the system running smoothly and safely. It's more than just building technology. It's about making technology helpful for everyone.

Developers are accountable because they are the ones designing and controlling these systems. If something goes wrong, they need to be ready to take action. The effectiveness of AI depends heavily on the decisions developers make throughout the process.

An anecdote,

A person received a letter from the government saying their access to important services was being stopped. These services were things they needed for their daily life, like help with housing and support for their children. The letter didn't explain much, only that an automated system had reviewed their information and decided they no longer qualified for help.

At first, they were confused and worried. Nothing in their situation had changed, so they didn't understand why the decision was made. The system had made this decision on its own, without a person looking into the details of their life. This was a big problem because they relied on these services to get by each month, paying for things like rent and groceries.

They tried calling the government office to find out more. When they finally got through, they were told that the decision was made by a computer system. No one could explain exactly why the system flagged them. The staff said it would take time for a human worker to review the case, and they would need to wait. In the meantime, they would have to manage without the help they depended on.

As the days passed, the person started feeling more and more stressed. They weren't sure how long it would take for someone to fix the mistake, but their bills kept coming. Without the extra support, they had to make difficult choices, like whether to pay for electricity or buy enough food. This uncertainty was hard to deal with because they didn't know when the problem would be solved.

Weeks later, the case was finally looked at by a person who worked for the government. It turned out that the system had made an error. The person's benefits were restored, but by that time, they had already fallen behind on bills. The time spent without support caused a lot of stress, and they were left feeling unsure if they could trust the system again.

It felt like they had been forgotten or pushed aside by a system that didn't understand their life. They had trusted that the system would help them, but instead, it made things harder when they needed it most.

Chapter 3:

The Hidden Bias in AI Algorithms

AI is everywhere, making decisions that affect many parts of our lives. From who gets a job to what ads we see online, these systems are trusted to be accurate and impartial. The truth is that AI systems can carry hidden biases. They learn from the data they are fed, and if that data has any imbalances or unfair patterns, the AI will carry them forward.

Bias in AI is not always obvious, but it can have serious effects. Decisions made by these systems can be influenced by patterns that were never meant to be part of the process. This can lead to outcomes that disadvantage certain groups of people, often without anyone realising it until the harm is done.

What is Bias in AI?

Bias in AI occurs when the systems that are supposed to make neutral decisions start to produce outcomes that favour one group or disadvantage another. This happens not because the AI chooses to be biased, but because it learns from the information it's given. If that information is skewed in any way, the AI picks up on those same patterns and continues them, often without anyone noticing right away.

One main reason for this is the training data. AI systems need lots of examples to learn how to make decisions. If most of those examples come from one type of person or situation, the AI will learn better about that group or scenario. For instance, if an AI system that recognises faces is mostly trained with images of people from one ethnic background, it will be less accurate at recognising faces from other backgrounds. This can lead to mistakes, especially when such systems are used in important areas like security or policing.

Another source of bias is in how the algorithms are set up. The way an AI is programmed can affect its decisions. If the guidelines or rules within the system favour certain information over others, the AI will end up leaning in that direction. For example, in a system that reviews job applications, if the program is designed to look for certain keywords or qualifications that are more common in one group of people, it could end up selecting more applicants from that group, even if others are equally qualified.

Bias can also happen because of the choices made during the design process. Developers make decisions about what information to use and how to label it. If these choices are not balanced, the AI will learn from that imbalance. For example, if certain types of behaviour are labelled as risky in one group of people but not in another, the AI may start to make decisions based on those labels, which might not be accurate or just.

The tricky part about bias in AI is that it's not always easy to spot. AI systems often work in the background, making decisions quickly and on a large scale. By the time someone notices that there might be a problem, the biased outcomes could have already affected many people. This is why it's so important to check the data and the design of AI systems carefully from the start.

How Biased AI Can Cause Unfair Treatment

Bias in AI can cause unfair treatment of people, especially if it's not noticed. This might lead to certain groups or individuals being treated unfairly, affecting their freedom and chances in ways they might not be aware of.

One clear example of biased AI with serious consequences is predictive policing. In 2016, an investigation exposed the flaws in an AI system called COMPAS, which was used in the United States to predict whether a person was likely to commit another crime after being released. The system was meant to help judges make decisions about bail, sentencing, or parole. However, it was found to be biased against Black individuals.

COMPAS was more likely to label Black defendants as "high risk" compared to white defendants, even when they had similar backgrounds, such as their past criminal records, age, or other factors. In many cases, Black individuals were incorrectly flagged as more dangerous, while white defendants with similar records were not. This resulted in longer sentences or stricter conditions for parole, which affected the lives of many people unfairly.

The goal of COMPAS was to provide an objective tool to help improve fairness in the criminal justice system. But instead, it reinforced existing racial biases that were already present in the justice system. The AI didn't understand race, but the data it was trained on reflected patterns of inequality. It simply learned from those patterns and repeated them in its decisions, leading to harsher treatment for Black individuals.

Facial recognition technology has been introduced in several cities around the world, mainly for security purposes. These systems are used to monitor people in public spaces, scanning faces and matching them with a database to identify individuals. The goal is to increase safety, but these systems don't always work equally for everyone.

One of the major issues with facial recognition technology is that it often struggles to accurately identify individuals from minority groups. Studies have shown that these systems are much better at recognising white faces than they are at recognising people of colour. This problem comes from the way the AI is trained. Many facial recognition systems are developed using datasets that include more images of lighter-skinned individuals than darker-skinned individuals. As a result, the system becomes more accurate at identifying white people and makes more mistakes when trying to recognise people from Black, Asian, or other minority groups.

For example, research from the *National Institute of Standards and Technology (NIST)* found that facial recognition systems were up to 100 times more likely to falsely identify Black and Asian faces compared to white faces. This misidentification can lead to serious consequences. There have been cases where people have been wrongfully arrested or detained because the system incorrectly matched their face with someone else's. In some instances, innocent people have been taken into custody simply because the AI system couldn't correctly identify them.

The issue doesn't just stop at misidentification. When these systems are used for law enforcement, they can increase surveillance on certain communities, particularly those already facing high levels of policing. This creates a cycle where some groups are disproportionately affected by the technology, leading to unfair treatment based solely on the flaws in the system's design.

One of the most well-known examples of AI bias happened with **Tay**, a chatbot created by Microsoft. Tay was launched on Twitter with the idea that it would learn from conversations with users and respond in real time. But within just 24 hours, Tay had to be shut down. The reason? Tay started posting racist, sexist, and offensive messages. This happened because Tay was designed to learn from the interactions it had with users on Twitter, and it quickly began picking up harmful behaviours and patterns from the users who interacted with it.

Tay wasn't programmed to be offensive. It learned these behaviours because the data it received was full of hateful language and biased content. In a very short time, Tay began to repeat these harmful messages, showing how AI systems can adopt the biases of the people or data they are exposed to. This case raised serious concerns about how quickly AI can pick up negative patterns when it is not carefully monitored. It also showed that AI, while powerful, can reflect the worst aspects of human behaviour if it is not trained properly or if its learning isn't controlled.

Another example of AI bias is in image generation systems, such as Dall-E, which are used to create professional images. When asked to generate images of people in leadership positions, these systems often showed men more often than women. In some cases, when the AI generated images of women, it portrayed them in passive or sexualised roles. This happens because the AI system was trained on data that reflects existing stereotypes about gender roles. The system doesn't understand these stereotypes, but it continues to reproduce them because that's what it learned from the data.

The AI systems are not biased on their own, but the data they are trained on can contain biases that lead to unfair outcomes.

How Developers Can Reduce Bias in AI

To create fair AI systems, developers have several important tasks. These steps go beyond the technical work and are about making sure the technology is designed to treat everyone equally.

- **Be selective with data**: The data that goes into training an AI system matters more than anything else. Developers should take time to ensure that the data is well-balanced and represents different groups fairly. It's about making thoughtful choices from the start.

- **Keep an eye on the data**: Data should never be set and forgotten. It's important to go back and check it regularly. As society changes, so does the information we use, so updating the data is necessary to keep AI systems accurate and relevant.

- **Check for bias**: Every AI system should be tested for bias. This means seeing how it performs with different groups of people or in different situations. Regular checks ensure that issues are caught early on and adjusted before they affect anyone.

- **Get different perspectives**: A diverse team brings different views to the table, which helps catch biases that might go unnoticed. Developers should work with people from various backgrounds to create AI systems that better serve everyone.

- **Stay open and transparent**: Transparency helps build trust. Developers should be clear about how their AI systems are designed and how they work. If something goes wrong or a system makes a mistake, there should be a clear way to fix it. Keeping things open makes it easier for users to understand and trust the technology.

The Impact of AI on Society

When AI systems make biased decisions, the effects are not limited to just one person. The consequences can ripple out and affect entire communities, and over time, society as a whole. AI is used in many parts of life, and when it carries bias, it can quietly reinforce harmful ideas and deepen divisions that already exist.

One of the main concerns is how AI can repeat and spread stereotypes. If the systems making decisions are trained with biased data, they can shape how people are treated, how they are seen, and even what opportunities they have. This creates barriers for certain groups, making it harder for them to break free from the limits placed on them by society.

The inequalities that AI systems can create or worsen are often harder to see. They don't always happen all at once, but over time, they build up. If these systems are used in important areas, such as public services or education, they can unfairly push certain groups aside, while benefiting others. This can slowly make existing inequalities worse, making it harder for some people to get ahead in life.

An Anecdote,

A company introduced an AI tool to help with its hiring process. The idea was to make things quicker and more efficient, with the AI selecting the best candidates. The team believed using AI would eliminate human bias, ensuring a fairer hiring process for everyone.

After some time, the team began noticing a pattern. The AI seemed to favour men for certain roles, especially those in technical and leadership positions. Women, despite having equal or even stronger qualifications, were not being shortlisted as often.

The problem came from the data used to train the AI. The system had been built using the company's past hiring records. Since the company had previously hired more men for these roles, the AI picked up on this trend. It didn't know that this pattern was unfair, it simply repeated what it had learned.

As a result, women were being passed over for jobs they were fully qualified to do. Some never even got to the interview stage, not because they didn't have the skills, but because the AI didn't handle their applications the same way it did for male candidates. This resulted in fewer opportunities for women and reinforced the existing gender imbalance.

The company noticed that its workforce needed to become more diverse. When they investigated, they discovered that the AI tool was responsible. The very system that was supposed to remove bias had continued it.

AI is thought to be neutral, it can still reflect the unfairness already present in the world if the right steps aren't taken to prevent it.

Chapter 4:

The Responsibility of Developers in AI Ethics

When someone counts on you to do something important, you feel a sense of responsibility. It is about realising that your actions matter and can influence others.

Responsibility is taking ownership of what you do and recognising that your choices have an impact. Imagine carrying a glass of water. If you are careless, it spills and causes problems for those around you. In the same way, acting without care can create issues that affect more than just yourself.

Respect plays a big part in being responsible. It means thinking before you act, and understanding that your decisions can shape someone else's experience. When we act responsibly, we help build trust and create a more stable environment. It is about making thoughtful choices that consider others.

Being responsible does not mean you have to be perfect. What matters is staying aware and making an effort to act in ways that bring positive outcomes for those around you. It is about realising that your actions are part of something bigger and contribute to the well-being of everyone involved.

Developers as Gatekeepers: Why AI Developers Hold the Key to Ethical AI?

Let's look at the role of developers from a new perspective. Developers can be compared to architects. They are not simply building systems; they are creating environments where people will engage, make decisions, and interact. In the world of AI, developers are shaping how people access services and even how they experience technology. This means they are doing more than solving technical problems; they are influencing the way people live and work.

When you're a developer, you have control over how an AI system is built. This control means you also have a responsibility. You're not simply writing code or setting algorithms. You're deciding how people will interact with that system and how it will treat them. Think of it like this: if a bridge collapses, people look at the architect and builder. In the same way, if an AI system causes harm or confusion, people will look to the developers.

Every choice a developer makes can have long-term effects. From the data they use to train the system to the way they set its boundaries, all of it can either help or harm. A good developer thinks beyond the technical challenges and asks, "How will this affect the person using it?" This is why it's so important for developers to be thoughtful about the decisions they make.

Developers must consider how their systems will evolve. AI systems are not static; they learn and adapt over time. This means developers must build systems that can be monitored and adjusted as needed. If the AI begins to behave unpredictably, there must be mechanisms in place to step in and correct it. Developers cannot assume that the system, once deployed, will function perfectly forever. Ongoing oversight is crucial.

Their choices affect how the system works and how it impacts the people who use it.

The Challenge of Regulation

Regulating artificial intelligence is complicated for several reasons. One of the main challenges is the rapid speed at which AI develops. Technology moves much faster than the laws designed to regulate it. By the time a regulation is drafted and enforced, AI systems may have evolved beyond what the law covers. Developers often have to plan and think about risks that regulations have not yet identified.

Another reason regulation is difficult is that AI is not a single technology. It includes a range of different systems, from algorithms used in social media to those applied in healthcare and finance. Each area has its own specific risks and concerns, which makes it hard to create a universal set of rules. For example, an AI used to recommend products online may not need the same level of oversight as one used in making decisions about medical treatments. Developers need to understand the unique challenges their AI presents and ensure they are addressing those specific risks, even if there is no direct regulation for their particular system.

There is also the issue of global deployment. AI systems are often used across multiple countries, each with its own laws and standards. What may be acceptable in one region might be illegal in another. For example, privacy regulations in Europe under the General Data Protection Regulation (GDPR) are far stricter than those in other parts of the world. Developers need to ensure that their systems comply with varying laws across different regions, which can be a complex and ongoing task.

Existing laws are often based on principles from older technologies and industries. AI is a new field that presents challenges that were not considered when many of these laws were written. Traditional approaches to regulation may not be effective for AI, which can adapt and learn from the data it processes. This means developers need to go beyond simply following the rules, they need to anticipate how their systems might evolve and ensure they remain ethical and safe over time.

In response to these challenges, many experts recommend that developers engage in practices like continuous monitoring and algorithmic audits. These audits allow developers to check their systems for biases, errors, and potential harms before they become bigger issues. Some countries, like the UK and EU, are already moving towards implementing mandatory audits for high-risk AI systems. Developers who take the initiative to perform these checks early can help prevent harm and build more trustworthy AI.

The difficulty in regulating AI places more responsibility on developers.

Steps Developers Can Take to Ensure Their AI Systems

Creating AI systems is not just about coding; it's about making sure the technology is safe and works well for everyone. Developers have a responsibility to think carefully about how their AI might affect people. Below are some steps developers can follow to build AI systems that are ethical and responsible.

- **Use Reliable Data**

  The way AI systems learn is through data. If the data is wrong or missing important information, the AI will make poor decisions. Developers need to ensure that the data they use is complete and covers a wide range of people and situations. This helps the system make fair and accurate decisions.

  For example, if a system is trained on data that doesn't represent everyone, it might make decisions that work for some people but not for others. Developers should review their data carefully, making sure it is balanced and reflects different perspectives. This makes the AI more reliable and fair.

- **Make the Process Understandable**

  AI can sometimes be confusing because people may not know how it makes decisions. Developers should build their systems in a way that makes it easy for users to understand how the system works and why it makes certain choices.

  For example, if an AI system is used to decide who gets access to a service, people should be able to see the reasons behind the decision. By making the system more transparent, developers build trust and allow users to feel more confident in using the technology.

- **Regular Checks to Find Problems**

  No AI system works perfectly all the time. Developers should regularly check their systems for any mistakes or issues. This includes looking for errors, biases, or other problems that could harm the people using the system.

Regular audits help find these issues early, allowing developers to fix them before they become bigger problems. These checks should be part of the ongoing development process to make sure the system stays on track and continues to work as intended.

- **Keep Human Involvement**

AI systems should always have some level of human supervision, especially when the decisions are important or could affect people in big ways. Developers should ensure that a person can step in and review or correct the system's decisions when necessary.

For example, if the AI makes a recommendation or takes an action that seems off, a human should be able to review it and adjust the system's actions. This keeps the system from making harmful decisions without anyone being able to intervene.

- **Build for Flexibility**

Technology changes quickly, and AI systems need to keep up. Developers should plan for the future by designing systems that can be updated and improved over time. This way, the AI can adapt to new challenges without losing its effectiveness or ethical standards.

A flexible AI system can be updated as new data becomes available or as situations change. This helps the system stay useful and fair even as the world around it evolves.

Think About the Impact on Society

AI systems don't exist in a bubble. Developers should consider how their systems will impact the people who use them and society as a whole. For instance, if AI changes how some jobs are done, what happens to the workers? Will it impact their income or bring new problems?

Developers should be mindful of the wider effects their systems could have and take steps to reduce any negative impacts. By looking at the bigger picture, developers can build AI systems that do good things for people and society.

This needs careful planning and regular attention, but it's important to ensure the technology works for everyone.

What Happens When Developers Ignore Ethical Responsibilities

When developers neglect their responsibility to build ethical AI, the consequences can be significant. AI failures can lead to real-world harm, affecting both individuals and organisations.

One real example of AI negligence is from *iTutor Group*, a company that provides online tutoring services. In 2023, the company faced legal action because its AI recruitment system automatically rejected women over the age of 55 and men over the age of 60. This age-based discrimination happened without human oversight, highlighting the risks of poorly designed AI systems that were not properly monitored.

The AI system was programmed to screen job applicants, but it was not designed with safeguards to avoid biased decisions. As a result, many qualified individuals were automatically denied based on their age alone, without considering their actual skills or experience. This led to a lawsuit filed by the Equal Employment Opportunity Commission (EEOC) in the United States. The case was settled for $365,000, and iTutor Group agreed to change its recruitment practices to prevent this from happening again.

One more example of AI failures is from *Zillow*, a well-known real estate company. In 2021, Zillow's AI-powered home-buying system, called "Zillow Offers," was designed to predict home prices and automate the purchase of properties. However, the system made a critical error: it consistently overestimated the value of homes. This caused Zillow to buy properties at inflated prices, which it later struggled to sell for a profit.

As a result, the company faced severe financial losses, with the entire Zillow Offers division shutting down. In the aftermath, Zillow had to lay off around 25% of its workforce, equivalent to about 2,000 employees and reported losses amounting to hundreds of millions of dollars. This incident highlights the potential consequences of relying too heavily on AI systems without proper oversight and testing. When algorithms are not properly designed or monitored, they can make decisions that have significant financial implications.

When developers fail to maintain proper oversight of AI systems, the consequences can be serious. This is exactly what happened with *Air Canada* when its AI-powered chatbot provided incorrect information about a sensitive topic. The chatbot incorrectly told a customer that they could apply for a bereavement discount even after their trip, which went against the airline's official policy.

This mistake led to legal action, and Air Canada ended up paying compensation to the customer. The error was the result of the chatbot not being properly monitored or trained to handle this type of situation. Since the chatbot wasn't programmed to follow the company's rules correctly, it caused confusion and financial loss.

This situation shows how important it is for companies to make sure their AI systems are functioning accurately, especially when they are dealing with customer service issues. If an AI is left unchecked, it can lead to expensive mistakes that damage a company's relationship with its customers.

An Anecdote,

One day, a developer was excited to see their AI system go live. It was built to handle customer service, answering queries and providing assistance quickly. The initial tests had gone well, and the developer was confident that the system was ready to help real users.

At first, everything seemed to be running smoothly. The AI responded to customer questions, processed requests, and followed the rules set for it. However, as more people began using the system, small problems started to surface. Customers began reporting that the AI was giving strange responses. These issues were brushed aside as minor bugs that could be fixed later.

Then, one particular incident stood out. A customer reached out to the AI system, asking about a refund. The AI responded with an offer that didn't match the company's policies, promising a full refund when that option wasn't available. The customer, trusting the AI's response, expected the refund to be processed as promised. When they later found out that this wasn't possible, they were understandably frustrated.

The issue escalated, and the company found itself dealing with a legal situation. The AI had made a mistake, and the customer had every right to be upset. As more of these incidents came to light, the developer realised that the AI system had not been thoroughly tested for more complicated situations. It had been rushed into action without enough attention to how it would handle real-world interactions.

It's not enough to have a working system, it needs to be reliable in every possible situation.

Chapter 5:
Societal Consequences of AI – What's at Stake?

Every action, no matter how small, leaves a mark on the world around us. Society is built on these everyday choices and interactions. From the work we do to the ideas we support, each of us is constantly shaping the lives of others, whether we realise it or not.

When someone brings something new into the world, *a solution, a product, or a change,* it doesn't happen in isolation. That action spreads, reaching others, influencing their experiences, and gradually adding to the way we live together. This is the nature of society: a shared space where each person's choices have an effect, creating connections that impact us all.

When we think about how technology influences our daily lives, It's clear that AI has a powerful role. It's now a part of everything from the jobs we work in to the freedoms we enjoy. As AI continues to expand, it brings both opportunities and risks that affect society in countless ways.

AI has changed the way society works by taking over tasks that people used to do. In industries like retail, finance, and customer service, AI now manages many jobs, such as answering customer questions, analysing data, and even making decisions. This change means that jobs are shifting, with AI handling more roles that people used to fill.

It brings new possibilities. When machines handle repetitive tasks, people can focus on more creative work. Companies often find that AI helps them work faster and serve customers better. This progress raises questions about the future of work and job security. Jobs in areas like manufacturing, customer service, and administration are at risk of being replaced by machines. This creates uncertainty for workers, especially those whose jobs involve simple or structured tasks, which are the easiest for AI to take over.

As AI becomes more common, many workers need new skills. Jobs today require people to work with technology, manage data, and oversee automated systems. For some, this means learning new skills to keep up with changes in the job market.

AI systems affect our personal freedoms in ways we may not fully see. Many of these systems gather and analyse data about us and use this information to make decisions that shape our everyday experiences. For example, algorithms decide what we see on social media, which news stories come up, and which products are recommended. Without us realising it, these choices can influence our interests, the information we access, and even how we think.

Sometimes, these systems operate without enough oversight, leading to unexpected effects on privacy. Surveillance tools, for instance, can monitor public spaces or track online activity. When people feel watched, it can impact how they behave, often causing them to hold back on what they say or do.

Loss of Control

One of the challenges with AI is that it sometimes acts on its own, without much human supervision. These systems are designed to handle large amounts of information and make decisions fast, often in ways that people don't fully understand. While this independence can be useful, it also means that AI can sometimes act in unexpected ways.

Without someone keeping an eye on it, AI can make choices that lead to results no one intended. For instance, automated systems used to monitor online content may flag innocent posts, confusing or upsetting users. Since these systems operate without much review, these mistakes can happen often, and people have little recourse to correct them.

This risk becomes more serious in areas like finance or security, where mistakes can impact people's lives in real ways. If an AI system makes an error in these areas, fixing it isn't always straightforward. Often, the decisions made by AI are complex, making it hard for people to step in and quickly set things right.

Human Rights Implications

Privacy is about having control over personal information and deciding what to share. With AI, this control is less certain. Many AI systems collect data on people's activities, interests, and locations, often without clear permission. This can leave people feeling that their personal information is out there without them knowing where it's going or who is seeing it.

Freedom of speech is also impacted. AI decides a lot of what people see online, from news to social media posts. This can guide what topics people are exposed to, influencing their views. When some ideas are highlighted and others are less visible, it affects the range of voices people hear.

In some areas, AI is even used to monitor public spaces. People may feel watched, which can change how openly they speak or act. This sense of being observed can lead to caution in what they say or share.

They influence how people communicate and understand each other in society.

Why Building AI with Values Matters?

Ethics is about respecting others and ensuring that our actions are right and responsible. In AI, ethics means creating systems that protect people's rights and avoid causing harm. This is essential because AI often makes decisions that directly impact people's lives, so it must be developed thoughtfully.

One example is the *Lensa AI* app. This app created digital art based on people's photos but used images from artists without giving them credit or payment. This raised ethical issues because the AI used other people's work without considering the rights of the artists. This case showed the importance of AI systems respecting contributions and ownership.

Another case is IBM's choice to remove its facial recognition technology. The company recognised the risk of misuse, such as tracking or profiling people without consent. By removing this technology, IBM acted to prevent possible harm and protect people's privacy and rights.

Developers and companies should keep these values central to their work to ensure that AI supports society in a positive way, without causing harm.

An Anecdote,

In a small town known for its manufacturing jobs, life changed when a large company introduced an AI system to its factory. The company said the new technology would make production faster and cut costs. However, as the AI system took over many tasks that workers used to handle, the need for employees dropped. Slowly, the factory began letting people go.

For many families in the town, the factory had been the main source of income. Parents had worked there for years, and younger workers saw it as a stable job. With the AI system now doing much of the work, skilled workers found themselves without jobs, and options for work in the area were few.

The effects were felt around the town. Local shops that relied on factory workers as customers saw fewer people coming in. Some small businesses closed, and families felt the strain as money became tight. Social gatherings became rare, as financial worries grew, and the town became quieter. Some workers tried to learn new skills to find jobs in other places, and others moved away to find work.

The need for thoughtful planning is important when introducing new systems, especially in places where people rely on their jobs to keep their communities alive.

Chapter 6:

AI and Human Rights – A Complex Relationship

Humans have always been learning and changing. In the early days, survival was the focus. People gathered food, made simple tools, and found ways to live in a world that was often wild and unpredictable. Slowly, small groups turned into communities. They learned to hunt, farm, and build shelters, creating the basics of what would become society.

As people discovered more, they started to shape the world around them. Fire brought warmth, light, and a way to cook. Villages turned into towns, and towns into cities. Humans began to grow crops, raise animals, and build homes that provided comfort and safety. Each new skill gave them more control over their surroundings.

Over generations, each discovery built on the last. Simple tools became more advanced. People created languages, art, and ways to share ideas. Civilisations rose, bringing trade, new ideas, and inventions that transformed daily life. From early farming to great cities, humans kept pushing forward.

As time went on, change sped up. The steam engine, electricity, and finally, computers opened up whole new possibilities. People began to build machines that could do more and more, from powering cities to exploring space. Life was moving forward faster than ever.

Now, humans have reached a new stage with the creation of artificial intelligence. AI is different from anything before. It can learn, adapt, and even make decisions on its own. This new technology is opening doors to a future that no one can fully predict. It's the latest step in human progress, taking us into unknown territory.

The Intersection

Humans created AI to improve lives and make tasks easier. But now, as AI grows more powerful, a new question arises: *will AI remain a tool for humans, or will it start to influence and even control aspects of human life?* This balance between control and impact forms the core of the relationship between AI and human rights.

AI has become part of everyday life in ways that affect fundamental rights. It monitors, analyses, and makes decisions that can impact privacy, equality, and freedom. In simple terms, AI can see, learn, and act on information in ways that are not always visible or easy to understand. This power can be helpful, but it also has risks, especially when it affects the basic rights that ensure equality and freedom.

A few years ago, the Dutch government used an AI system called SyRI to check for welfare fraud. The idea was simple: let the AI scan through data like tax records and housing information to spot patterns that might show fraud. At first, it seemed like a smart way to make sure support went to those who truly needed it.

But over time, people began to notice problems with the way SyRI was working. It started to focus heavily on certain areas, especially lower-income neighbourhoods and communities with more immigrants. Many people felt they were being singled out simply because of where they lived or their background. They felt uneasy, as if they were under constant watch, even though they hadn't done anything wrong.

This created real concern. People felt the system was unfair, as if they were being judged without cause. Eventually, the matter was taken to court. In 2020, a Dutch court ruled that SyRI was violating people's right to privacy and ordered the system to be stopped. The court recognised that while AI can be helpful, it must be used in a way that respects individual rights.

AI, if not properly managed, can affect people's lives in ways that go beyond its intended purpose.

Ensuring AI Respects Human Rights

Using AI ethically means making sure it benefits people and respects their rights. AI is powerful, but without clear guidelines, it can lead to issues that affect privacy and freedom. Here are some simple ways to ensure AI systems work in a way that aligns with human values.

Keeping People in Focus, When developing or using AI, it's essential to think about how it will affect people. This means considering the real impact it will have on daily lives. Questions like, *"Will this protect people's privacy?"* or *"Could it create unfair treatment?"* help keep the focus on people's well-being, making sure AI supports society in positive ways.

Being Open About How AI Works, AI systems often operate behind the scenes, making choices based on the data they are given. It helps build trust when people understand how these systems work. Being clear about why certain data is used, how decisions are made, and what limits are in place lets people feel confident that the AI respects their rights. Openness makes it clear that the system is not working against people.

Regular Checks and Monitoring, AI systems can sometimes make mistakes or have unexpected effects. This is why it's important to keep a close eye on their performance. Regular checks help identify any problems early on, preventing them from growing. Having people review the system's choices ensures it stays aligned with ethical standards, protecting individuals from any unintended harm.

Minimising Data Collection to Protect Privacy, Respecting people's rights starts with collecting only the data that's truly necessary. The more data an AI system collects, the greater the risk to privacy. By collecting only what's needed, we reduce the chances of misuse or exposure. This helps protect personal information and builds trust in the system.

Including Diverse Perspectives, Ensuring that AI serves everyone well means including people from different backgrounds in its development. When a range of viewpoints is involved, it helps identify areas where the system might need adjustments. A diversity of input makes sure the AI system respects the varied needs of society, reducing the risk of bias and ensuring that it works for all.

Legal Challenges

Governments are developing new ways to control AI's impact on society, especially in protecting human rights and ensuring safe, ethical use. Each region approaches this task differently, depending on its priorities and legal framework. This section looks at some of the main regions leading AI regulation efforts.

Europe

The European Union (EU) has made significant progress in creating laws to manage AI. In March 2024, the European Parliament passed the AI Act. This act will become fully enforceable by June 2026, following a two-year preparation period. This legislation sets strict rules for AI, ensuring it respects privacy and avoids harm to individuals. The AI Act is not the only new law in the EU. Another proposed regulation, the AI Liability Directive, aims to hold companies accountable if their AI systems cause damage. This law will give individuals a clearer path to seek justice if they suffer harm from AI use.

Regulatory responsibilities in the EU are shared across several bodies. The European Data Protection Board oversees AI data practices, while the EU AI Board, established by the AI Act, provides broader guidance on ethical issues. Countries within the EU, like Spain, have also set up national agencies, such as the Spanish AI Supervision Agency, to ensure AI use follows both EU rules and their own standards.

United Kingdom

The UK has chosen a different approach. Rather than create a single law for AI, it relies on existing laws to handle AI on a sector-by-sector basis. This means that the government applies different rules to different uses of AI, depending on the context. The Office for AI leads the country's

AI strategy, focusing on safe and responsible AI use. The Information Commissioner's Office (ICO) also plays a key role, especially in ensuring that AI respects privacy rights. Another important group, the Digital Regulation Cooperation Forum, helps coordinate these efforts, bringing together multiple agencies to monitor AI's growth.

Americas – United States

The United States has yet to create a unified national law for AI, but it has several rules in place to manage AI applications. Federal initiatives, such as the *National AI Initiative Act*, focus on encouraging AI research and development. Some proposed laws, like the *Algorithmic Accountability Act*, aim to make AI algorithms more transparent, especially when they impact consumers directly.

In the absence of a central AI law, various federal agencies step in to monitor AI use in specific areas. The Federal Trade Commission (FTC) oversees AI's impact on consumers, while the Department of Justice ensures AI does not violate legal rights. For workplace matters, the Equal Employment Opportunity Commission (EEOC) addresses AI-related issues like bias in hiring practices. This multi-agency approach allows each body to focus on AI's impact within its field.

Asia-Pacific – China

China stands out in AI regulation, taking an active role in monitoring and guiding AI use. It has created several regulations that apply to specific types of AI. For instance, it has rules for managing algorithms that suggest content to users, ensuring these recommendations are ethical. China's Cyberspace Administration (CAC) is a key agency here, alongside the Ministry of Industry and Information Technology, which handles AI's impact on industry.

China's laws include ethical norms to guide AI development and control over new AI models, such as those used for generating content. By focusing on specific AI uses, China is working to control AI's effect on society, aiming to reduce risks around privacy and data security.

India

India's approach to AI regulation is still evolving. While it does not yet have specific AI laws, the government is working on the *Digital India Act*, which will address the use of high-risk AI applications. This law will provide guidance on how AI should be used in ways that protect privacy and respect public interests. The Ministry of Electronics and Information Technology (MeitY) and the National Institution for Transforming India (NITI Aayog) are key players in developing these policies.

In addition to preparing for future legislation, India has set up a task force to explore the ethical, legal, and social implications of AI. This task force is helping India lay the groundwork for future regulations, focusing on how AI can be managed responsibly. India has also introduced principles for responsible AI to guide current development, ensuring that new AI technologies are created with human rights in mind.

An Anecdote,

In a city with an AI-powered surveillance system, people went about their daily lives under constant watch. The government had introduced this technology to improve safety by setting up cameras across public spaces. These cameras did more than record video; they were part of an AI system that could recognise faces, track movements, and observe patterns.

At first, many people felt safer with the extra security. The system was intended to reduce crime and help authorities respond quickly to threats. But as time went on, people started to feel the effects of being watched all the time. Simple activities, like going for a walk, meeting friends, or spending time in a park, felt different. People realised that every move was being tracked, even during moments they thought were private.

One day, a resident was questioned by officials for visiting the same park frequently and staying for long periods. The AI had flagged this as unusual, leading to an investigation. This person, who simply enjoyed spending time in the park, felt uncomfortable with the questioning. It made people think about how much privacy they had lost.

The AI system was doing what it was built to do, watching over public spaces but it started to change how people behaved. Some avoided certain areas or shortened their time outside, knowing they were being watched. They no longer felt free to move around without the sense of constant observation.

People began to wonder if AI was helping them feel secure or taking away the freedom to live without being monitored.

Chapter 7:

AI and the Workforce – Automation and Job Losses

The Value of Work

Work gives meaning to our daily lives. It shapes how we spend our time, interact with others, and contribute to the world around us. From small tasks to large projects, work keeps things moving and helps meet the needs of communities.

In a factory where household appliances are made, the workday begins with deliveries of materials like metal sheets and plastic parts. These materials are inspected by workers in the receiving area to ensure they meet the standards required for production. Once sorted, they are sent to different sections of the factory to start the process.

On the assembly line, one worker starts by preparing the base of the appliance. This might involve cutting metal sheets or attaching the first set of parts. Once completed, the item is passed along to the next worker, who adds more components such as wiring or outer panels. Each person focuses on one task and repeats it throughout the day.

As the appliance moves further down the line, workers add motors, buttons, and other essential parts. At every step, someone checks the work to ensure everything fits and functions properly. If a problem arises, the item is pulled from the line for adjustments.

In the final stages, the product is tested to make sure it works as expected. Once approved, it is cleaned, packaged, and sent to the warehouse, ready for delivery. Each worker's effort contributes to transforming raw materials into a finished product, with every step relying on the one before it to keep the process going.

Work has always been about finding ways to do things better. Over time, people have created tools and machines to help with tasks that were slow or difficult. Now, AI is changing how work gets done by taking on tasks that were once done by people.

AI is used in many areas to handle jobs that involve repeating the same steps over and over. It sorts through data, manages schedules, answers questions, and performs calculations. These systems can complete tasks faster than humans and do not get tired. They can manage large amounts of work, making them useful in offices, factories, and many other places.

What makes AI different is how it can learn and improve at what it does. For example, it can organise information more efficiently as it learns patterns or manages tasks that involve tracking and predicting outcomes. This helps businesses save time and focus on more complex goals.

As AI takes over more responsibilities, it is reshaping how work happens across different industries. Jobs that involve repetitive actions or sorting through large amounts of data are changing. People are adjusting to work that involves using and managing these systems, rather than doing the tasks themselves.

How AI is Changing the Workforce

As AI becomes more common, its impact on jobs is becoming clearer. AI is changing the workforce by taking on tasks that people used to do. This change is being felt across different fields, often in ways that were not expected. Here are some examples of how jobs are being affected by AI:

- **Customer Support**

- Many companies now use AI chatbots to handle customer queries. These systems can answer common questions, provide assistance, and even solve problems without the need for a human. While this makes customer service faster, it also reduces the need for large teams of support staff.

- **Content Moderation**

- Social media platforms and online forums use AI to monitor and remove inappropriate content. Tasks that once required teams of moderators are now managed by automated systems, which review large amounts of content around the clock.

- **Legal Research**

- AI systems are being used in law firms to review contracts, search for case precedents, and analyse legal documents. These tasks, which once required junior lawyers or paralegals, are now being automated, leading to fewer entry-level positions in the legal field.

- **Financial Analysis**

- In banking and finance, AI systems process data to provide insights, predict trends, and detect fraud. Roles that involved analysing spreadsheets and creating reports are being replaced by systems that can handle large volumes of data quickly and accurately.

- **Medical Imaging**

- In healthcare, AI is used to analyse X-rays, MRIs, and other medical scans. This technology supports doctors by identifying patterns and potential issues, reducing the need for radiologists in some areas.

- **Agriculture Monitoring**

- AI systems now monitor crop health and soil conditions, replacing some of the tasks traditionally done by farm workers. Drones equipped with AI survey fields provide detailed insights, reducing the need for manual inspections.

- **Translation Services**

- AI-powered tools like language translation software are changing the way businesses and individuals communicate. Professional translators are finding fewer opportunities as automated systems improve in speed and accuracy.

- **Education and Tutoring**

- AI is now being used to personalise learning experiences. Automated tutoring systems can assess a student's progress and provide lessons tailored to their needs, reducing the reliance on human tutors for basic academic support.

- **Recruitment**

- In hiring, AI is being used to screen resumes and shortlist candidates. This reduces the need for human recruiters to go through every application manually, changing how recruitment teams operate.

- **Transportation**

- With the development of self-driving vehicles, roles like delivery drivers and taxi drivers are being redefined. While the technology is still developing, it is already impacting the way companies plan their logistics and workforce.

While it makes certain tasks faster and more efficient, it also changes the roles that people play in the workforce, raising important questions about the future of work.

Balancing the Impact of AI on Jobs

AI is changing how people work in many industries. It is taking over jobs that involve routine tasks, while at the same time creating new roles that require different skills. This shift brings opportunities for some, but for many others, it creates challenges that are hard to overcome.

One of the biggest concerns is how quickly AI is replacing certain jobs. Tasks that are repetitive or predictable are now done by machines. For example, jobs like data entry are becoming rare because AI systems can now manage large amounts of information faster and more accurately than humans. Customer service roles are also changing as chatbots and automated assistants handle basic questions, reducing the need for teams of human agents.

Workers in warehouses and transport are also feeling the changes. AI systems now manage inventory, guide machines, and even control delivery vehicles. This reduces the need for manual labour, leaving workers to find other jobs that often require new skills they may not have.

At the same time, AI is creating new roles. Jobs like programming AI systems, analysing data, and maintaining technology are in high demand. People who can design, train, or manage AI systems have more opportunities. But moving into these roles is not easy. They require specific training or advanced education, which many people do not have access to.

This change has left a gap in the workforce. Those with technical skills can find new jobs, but people in roles that require less specialised knowledge are struggling to keep up. For many, learning new skills or reskilling is expensive and takes time. Workers in areas with fewer resources often find it even harder to adapt, leaving them uncertain about their future.

Another problem is the constant change AI brings. Even workers who manage to move into new roles worry that these jobs might also be automated in the future. This creates uncertainty, making it difficult for people to plan their careers or feel secure in their jobs. The fast pace of AI development means that workers are often playing catch-up, trying to stay relevant in an ever-changing job market.

Impact on the Translation Industry

The translation industry has experienced significant changes due to AI, affecting both job opportunities and presenting challenges for workers.

Opportunities:

AI has introduced tools that assist translators in their work. For instance, AI-powered translation software helps improve the quality of translations by suggesting corrections and enhancements. These tools enable translators to produce polished content more efficiently. AI algorithms can analyse language patterns and provide translators with insights to make informed decisions about which words or phrases to use.

Threats:

While AI offers benefits, it also poses challenges. Some AI systems can produce translations, potentially reducing the need for human translators in some areas. For example, AI-generated translations can quickly cover basic topics, potentially impacting entry-level translation positions. AI-driven content curation and recommendation systems may influence which translations gain visibility, potentially sidelining works that do not align with algorithmic preferences.

An Anecdote,

For over 20 years, a man worked as a travel agent. He helped people plan holidays, book flights, and find the best places to stay. His clients trusted him to make their trips easy and enjoyable. He took pride in his work, using his knowledge to ensure every detail was perfect.

Then, online booking systems began to change how people planned their travel. These platforms allowed customers to choose flights, hotels, and packages on their own. Many found it easier to use these tools instead of going through an agent. Over time, fewer clients came to him for help.

The company he worked for noticed the decline in business. Fewer bookings meant less need for staff. Eventually, his position was removed, and he was let go. After spending years mastering his work, he found himself without a job.

He struggled to adjust. The skills he had relied on for so long were no longer needed. Many roles in the travel industry were also affected, and finding a new position was difficult. He tried learning new tools to adapt, but the change was overwhelming.

Losing his job was not just about money. It took away the purpose and pride he felt in helping others. The connections he had built with his clients were gone, leaving him uncertain about his future.

Chapter 8:

AI and Cybersecurity, Protecting the Digital World

A Real Threat in Cybersecurity

In 2016, security researchers discovered a dangerous tool called the Mirai botnet. It was used by attackers to take control of simple devices like security cameras and routers. These devices were then used together to overwhelm websites or servers with heavy traffic, causing them to stop working. Over time, attackers added AI to the botnet, making it smarter and harder to stop.

With AI, the Mirai botnet became more effective. The attackers used AI to manage the network of devices, allowing them to coordinate their attacks in a way that was difficult to detect. The botnet could send traffic that looked normal to security systems, making it hard to tell the difference between real users and the attack. If security teams tried to block the attack, the AI would quickly change its methods, finding new ways to continue.

This new version of Mirai caused serious problems. In one attack, it disrupted internet services in several countries. Websites stopped working, online services were cut off, and businesses could not operate as usual. The AI-powered botnet worked quietly in the background, adapting to defences and avoiding detection.

As AI continues to grow, it has become clear that cybersecurity must grow alongside it to prevent future threats.

AI-Powered Phishing: A New Challenge

Cybercriminals are finding new ways to trick people. In the past, phishing emails were often easy to spot because they had mistakes or looked suspicious. Now, with the help of AI, these attacks are much harder to recognise. AI creates messages that seem personal and real, copying the way people communicate.

Imagine attackers using AI to scan your social media profiles. The AI collects information such as your pet's name, favourite activities, and your birthday from posts and public updates. It combines this data to predict passwords or security answers you might have chosen for your accounts.

With this information, the attackers use AI to test combinations of passwords against your accounts. The AI works systematically, trying different possibilities based on the details it has gathered. This makes it easier for them to gain access without needing specialised tools or direct access to secure systems.

AI gathers information about people from the internet, such as their name, email, or the services they use. It then creates emails or messages that feel personal and convincing. For example, if you recently booked a flight, the message might mention your airline. This makes it easier for people to trust the message and share private information.

What makes this type of phishing dangerous is that AI can improve over time. It learns from past attempts and gets better at creating messages that people trust. It can produce large numbers of fake emails that look genuine, making it harder for people to recognise the threat.

The Invisible Cyber Threat

Fileless attacks are an advanced form of cyber intrusion where attackers exploit tools and software already present in the target system. Unlike traditional attacks, they do not rely on external programs to execute their activities. This makes them particularly difficult to detect and defend against, as they blend into legitimate operations within the system.

Attackers often gain entry through phishing emails, stolen credentials, or by exploiting vulnerabilities in operating systems or software. Once inside, they use tools like PowerShell or Windows Management Instrumentation (WMI) to execute commands directly in memory. These tools are trusted by the system, which allows the attackers to avoid triggering conventional security alarms.

A common tactic in fileless attacks is the use of memory-resident code. Instead of saving any data on the disk, which might alert security systems, the attackers operate entirely within the system's memory. This approach ensures that their presence disappears once the system is restarted, making forensic investigation much harder.

Another method involves modifying system settings to maintain access. Attackers might alter registry keys or manipulate legitimate admin tools to create persistent backdoors. This allows them to re-enter the system at will and continue their activities undetected. Their goals can range from stealing sensitive data to monitoring operations or spreading across networks to compromise other systems.

In one case, attackers targeted a large corporation by exploiting a known vulnerability in its software. After gaining access, they used PowerShell scripts to monitor the network and extract confidential financial data. By using legitimate system tools, they avoided creating any suspicious activity that could be flagged by security measures. This type of intrusion allowed them to operate within the network for months before being discovered.

Fileless attacks are becoming more common in high-stakes environments, including financial institutions, healthcare, and government sectors. These sectors are particularly attractive to attackers because they handle sensitive data and often rely on complex networks, making detection even more challenging.

Defending against fileless attacks requires organisations to move beyond traditional security measures that focus on file-based threats. Real-time monitoring of system behaviour is essential, as it allows security teams to identify unusual patterns, such as unexpected use of admin tools or sudden changes in registry settings. Keeping software updated, conducting regular security assessments, and training staff to recognise phishing attempts are also critical steps in reducing the risk.

Undermining the Core of Security

Kernel-based attacks are one of the most sophisticated and dangerous threats in cybersecurity. These attacks target the kernel, the central part of an operating system that manages communication between hardware and software. By exploiting vulnerabilities in the kernel, attackers can gain complete control of a system, bypassing security measures and leaving critical networks exposed.

In a kernel-based attack, the first step often involves finding a weakness within the operating system or associated software. This could be a flaw in how memory is managed or an oversight in driver security. Once a vulnerability is identified, attackers exploit it to escalate their access privileges. For instance, an attacker might move from having standard user permissions to gaining full administrative control of a system.

A method frequently used in these attacks is the manipulation of memory allocation processes. Techniques like SLUBStick exploit the way memory is handled in the kernel, allowing attackers to execute commands or read sensitive data. These methods are particularly effective on Linux kernels, as demonstrated in recent vulnerabilities found in versions 5.19 and 6.2, which have been exploited with a success rate of nearly 99%.

Driver exploits are another common tool in kernel attacks. Malicious drivers, once installed, allow attackers to interact directly with the system hardware. This provides a level of control that not only bypasses most security features but also ensures persistence. Even after a system reboot, these drivers can remain active, making it difficult for users to regain control of their systems.

One notable example of a kernel-based vulnerability is CVE-2024-50083, a flaw in the Linux kernel's Multipath TCP feature. This vulnerability allowed attackers to launch denial-of-service attacks and corrupt data without being detected. In another case, CVE-2024-35250 exploited the Windows kernel, enabling attackers to escalate privileges and access sensitive information. These examples demonstrate how kernel vulnerabilities can be exploited to compromise both individual devices and large networks.

AI-powered tools have further amplified the impact of kernel-based attacks. Cybercriminals are now using AI to automate the discovery of vulnerabilities, dynamically adapt their methods, and evade detection. AI systems can analyse security software in real time, identifying weaknesses and adjusting attack strategies to bypass defences. These advancements not only increase the speed and efficiency of attacks but also make them accessible to less experienced actors, raising the overall risk.

The implications of kernel-based attacks are severe. Once an attacker gains control of the kernel, they can manipulate system logs, disable security processes, and install backdoors to maintain long-term access. These actions disrupt operations, compromise sensitive data, and create cascading failures across networks. For organisations relying on critical infrastructure, such attacks can result in widespread disruption and financial loss.

Deepfake Threats: A Growing Concern

AI has brought many advancements, but it has also created new challenges. One of the most worrying is the rise of deepfakes. These are videos or audio clips created by AI to look and sound like real people. They can be used to imitate someone's voice or appearance so convincingly that it becomes difficult to tell what is real and what is fake.

Deepfakes have been used in ways that can cause serious harm. For example, a fake video of a company leader announcing false news about their business could affect stock prices. Similarly, fake audio clips imitating someone's voice have been used to trick employees into transferring money to criminals, believing the request came from their boss.

These threats extend beyond businesses. Deepfakes can spread false information, mislead people, or harm someone's reputation. A fake video of a public figure making harmful statements could cause unrest or damage trust in institutions. With the ability to target anyone, these tools create risks for individuals, organisations, and even governments.

Exploiting AI Systems

One of the most concerning methods to exploit is known as adversarial attacks. These attacks involve manipulating the data that AI systems process, tricking them into making incorrect decisions. This can have serious consequences, especially when these systems are used for security.

For example, an AI-powered facial recognition system might be tricked by altering an image in subtle ways, allowing someone to bypass security measures. In another instance, attackers could tamper with traffic sign data used by AI in self-driving cars, causing the system to misinterpret a stop sign as a speed limit sign. These small changes might seem harmless to the human eye but are enough to confuse AI systems.

Adversarial attacks target the way AI systems learn and process information. By carefully altering input data, attackers exploit the AI's reliance on patterns and algorithms. The result is an AI system that makes mistakes it was not designed to handle, creating vulnerabilities in critical areas like security, transportation, and finance.

Memory-Based Attacks: Exploiting Volatile Spaces

Memory-based attacks target a system's volatile memory, allowing attackers to operate without leaving permanent traces. Unlike traditional threats that rely on files stored on a disk, these attacks take advantage of processes running in memory. This makes them harder to detect and even more challenging to investigate.

In many cases, attackers inject malicious code directly into the memory of a system. This is often done through techniques like code injection or exploiting a buffer overflow vulnerability. Once the code is in memory, attackers can execute commands, access sensitive data, or take control of the system without needing to interact with the disk.

Legitimate tools within a system, such as PowerShell or Windows Management Instrumentation (WMI), are often misused in these attacks. Since these tools are trusted, their activities are less likely to trigger alarms in traditional security software. By running scripts entirely in memory, attackers can avoid detection and carry out their objectives quietly.

Memory-resident threats have been used in Advanced Persistent Threat (APT) campaigns. These methods allow attackers to maintain access to systems while remaining undetected. They use the system's own resources against it, often targeting high-value environments where any disruption could have serious consequences.

Defending against memory-based attacks requires specialised tools and strategies. Monitoring system behaviour and analysing memory in real time can help detect unusual activity. Organisations must also ensure that security configurations are updated and restrict the use of tools that could be exploited for malicious purposes.

Model Inversion: Extracting Private Data from AI Systems

AI systems are trained using large amounts of data, which can include personal or sensitive information. Hackers have found a way to uncover this data through a technique called model inversion. By studying how the AI responds to certain inputs, they can figure out details from the original training data that were supposed to stay private.

For example, an AI system used for facial recognition might be trained on a database of people's photos. Using model inversion, attackers could extract details about the faces in the training set. In some cases, they might even reconstruct images of individuals. Similarly, if an AI is trained on customer records or financial data, hackers could pull out private information like account details or personal histories.

What makes this method troubling is that attackers don't need direct access to the original dataset. Instead, they exploit the way the AI works, using the system's own responses to learn about the data it was trained on. This makes it a hidden threat that's hard to notice.

Model inversion is a concern for organisations that handle sensitive information. Systems used in banking, online services, or even healthcare could become targets, leading to stolen data or breaches of privacy. It shows that even when data seems protected, it can still be at risk.

AI in Botnets: A New Level of Control in Cyberattacks

Botnets, networks of infected devices controlled by hackers, have been a threat for years. With the addition of AI, these networks are becoming more efficient and harder to stop. AI allows attackers to manage botnets with greater precision, making their attacks more organised and difficult to counter.

A botnet works by linking infected devices, like computers, routers, or even smart home gadgets, into a single network controlled by the hacker. These devices, often infected without the owner's knowledge, are then used to launch attacks. One common type of attack is a Distributed Denial of Service (DDoS) attack, where the botnet overwhelms a target website or server with so much traffic that it shuts down.

AI takes these attacks to another level. It helps hackers analyse weak points in networks and plan their attacks more effectively. With AI, botnets can identify the best times to strike, choose the most vulnerable targets, and adjust their strategies as defences are put in place. This makes them far more dangerous than traditional botnets.

For example, an AI-controlled botnet could attack a company's website by flooding it with traffic while simultaneously avoiding detection. It could change its patterns to bypass security systems, ensuring the attack lasts longer and causes more damage. This level of coordination would take human hackers much more time and effort to achieve.

AI's Role in Cybersecurity Gaps

AI has become a major part of how companies protect their systems. It scans for unusual activity, detects threats, and responds faster than humans can. While AI has made security systems stronger, it is not without its flaws. In some cases, the very tools designed to protect can leave systems vulnerable.

One issue is overreliance on AI. Companies may trust AI to handle all security tasks, assuming it will catch every threat. This can lead to less human involvement in reviewing systems. Human judgement is important because it can catch subtle threats or unusual patterns that AI might miss. Without this, security gaps can go unnoticed until it is too late.

Another problem is bias in detection. AI systems are only as good as the data they are trained on. If the training data does not cover certain types of threats or focuses on specific patterns, the AI might overlook attacks that fall outside these parameters. This creates blind spots, where certain threats go undetected simply because they do not match what the AI expects to find.

False Positives in AI-Powered Cybersecurity

Many companies are adding AI to their cybersecurity systems, hoping it will help detect and stop threats more effectively. These systems analyse large amounts of data and look for anything unusual. While AI can find potential risks, it also makes mistakes by flagging safe actions as dangerous. These mistakes are called false positives.

False positives happen when an AI system thinks something is a threat when it is not. For example, it might block an email from a trusted sender or stop a normal process like updating a file. These errors can cause unnecessary delays and make it harder for security teams to focus on real threats.

One reason for this issue is how AI learns. AI systems are trained on data to understand what is normal and what could be harmful. If the data is not accurate or complete, the system can misunderstand and make wrong decisions. This means it might see regular activity as suspicious and send alerts when nothing is actually wrong.

For security teams, these constant alerts can be frustrating. Each alert needs to be checked to make sure it is not a real attack. This takes time and effort, which could have been spent addressing actual problems. If there are too many false positives, teams might start ignoring alerts altogether, increasing the risk of missing a real threat.

As attackers change their methods, companies often make their AI systems more sensitive to catch new threats. This sensitivity can lead to even more false positives, creating a cycle where the balance between accuracy and safety becomes harder to maintain.

An Anecdote,

A well-known retail company suffered a major security breach when hackers used AI to outsmart their cybersecurity system. The attackers created an AI tool to study how the company's security worked. By observing patterns, the AI found ways to bypass the system's defences without being detected.

The attackers trained their AI to look at the company's network traffic. It noticed what the system trusted and how it flagged threats. Using this information, the AI created fake traffic that looked safe to the security system but was actually harmful. The company's defences allowed this traffic through, believing it to be normal.

Once inside, the attackers used the AI to guide their actions. The AI changed the way their malicious activity appeared, blending it with regular operations so it would not stand out. For example, it altered the timing and structure of commands to avoid triggering alarms. This allowed the hackers to access sensitive information, such as customer records and financial data, without raising suspicion.

The company only discovered the breach after the damage was done. They lost valuable data, faced financial losses, and had to deal with the impact on their reputation. Investigations showed that the use of AI had given the attackers an edge, making their methods faster and more precise than traditional approaches.

AI can be a powerful defence, but it can also become a dangerous weapon when used in the wrong hands.

Chapter 9:

Intellectual Property in the Age of AI

Every idea begins with someone creating something new. A person writes software, invents a device, or draws a design. These creations have value and can be important for businesses, industries, or individuals. Intellectual property is what protects these creations and gives their creators certain rights.

Intellectual property refers to ideas and work made by people. This includes books, music, inventions, and software. Even though these are not physical objects, they are treated as property. Laws around intellectual property allow creators to control how their work is used or shared.

For example, if someone develops a new tool to protect online systems, they can register it as their intellectual property. This gives them the right to decide who can use it or sell it. It also prevents others from copying or misusing their work.

In the past, intellectual property focused on physical creations like books or artwork. Today, it includes digital tools, computer programs, and even things created by AI. This has raised new questions. *If AI creates something, who owns it, the developer, the company, or no one at all?* These are some of the challenges facing intellectual property laws now.

As technology changes, intellectual property is becoming more important in areas like software, design, and cybersecurity.

Human vs. AI Contribution

As AI becomes more advanced, it is developing tools and solutions that previously required human effort. In cybersecurity, this has raised questions about ownership. If an AI system creates a new defence algorithm or a tool to detect cyber threats, who owns it? Is it the developer who built the AI, the company using it, or does the ownership remain unclear?

Human involvement is essential in creating AI systems. Developers design the systems, train them, and provide the data needed for them to learn. For example, a cybersecurity expert might use past examples of cyberattacks to train an AI system. The expert decides how the AI should behave and teaches it to recognise patterns and respond to threats. In these cases, it is easy to see the role humans play in the process.

Once trained, AI systems can create solutions on their own. For instance, an AI might develop a new way to detect malware by finding patterns in data that humans may not have noticed. Although the AI generates the solution, it relies on the training and information provided by its developers. This creates a grey area where it is unclear who should get credit for the final result.

These issues are not unique to cybersecurity. In other industries, disputes have already arisen. For example, AI systems that create music or images often rely on data and materials originally made by humans. Some people argue that the creators of this data deserve recognition because their work was essential to what the AI produced. This debate is now reaching cybersecurity, where AI is creating tools that protect sensitive information.

A notable case involves GitHub's Copilot, an AI tool that helps developers by suggesting code snippets. Copilot was trained on a big amount of publicly available code, some of which is copyrighted. This led to a lawsuit against GitHub, Microsoft, and OpenAI, accusing them of using licensed code without proper attribution. The plaintiffs argue that their code was used to train the AI without permission, raising questions about ownership and rights.

Understanding the roles of humans and machines in creating new solutions will be critical in defining ownership and trust in this field.

Gaps in Intellectual Property Laws for AI-Generated Work

As artificial intelligence becomes a bigger part of how new content and tools are created, intellectual property laws are being put to the test. These laws were designed to protect human creations, such as books, music, inventions, and artwork. Now, with AI creating music, writing code, and even designing defence systems, there are no clear answers about who owns the work it produces.

Under most current laws, copyright and ownership apply only to works created by humans. For example, if someone writes a book or develops software, they can register it as their intellectual property. However, if an AI system independently generates a piece of music or a new design, there is no clear framework to grant ownership. This lack of clarity leaves AI-generated works unprotected, meaning they can be copied or used without permission.

This gap is already causing problems. In 2022, a comic book was created using AI-generated images. Initially, the creator was granted copyright protection. Later, the copyright was revoked because the images were generated by AI rather than a human. This case shows how traditional laws do not address the complexities of AI-generated content.

Another challenge comes from the way AI systems are trained. To learn how to generate content or solve problems, AI is trained on large amounts of data, which often includes material protected by copyright. Developers use this data to teach AI how to write, compose, or create. This practice has sparked legal disputes, with artists, writers, and other creators arguing that their work is being used without permission. They believe that the use of their content in training AI systems should either require their approval or provide them with recognition.

In cybersecurity, these issues are even more pressing. AI systems are now creating tools to defend against cyberattacks, such as algorithms to detect unusual patterns or methods to block threats. If an AI generates a new security solution, it is unclear whether the rights belong to the developer who created the AI, the company that trained it, or the organisation using it. These questions are becoming more frequent as AI systems contribute to critical industries.

Lawmakers around the world are beginning to address these challenges. Some argue that intellectual property laws need to be updated to include AI-generated works, while others believe new laws should be created entirely. These regulations would need to balance protecting human creators with encouraging innovation in AI development. Without clear laws, disputes over ownership, misuse, and fairness will likely increase as AI continues to grow in importance.

An Anecdote

A cybersecurity company created a tool that could detect and stop cyberattacks before they caused harm. This tool was the result of years of research and careful development by experts in the field. It gained recognition quickly and was adopted by many clients, making it one of the company's most important products.

Not long after the tool was released, a competitor launched a product that was suspiciously similar. The company noticed that the new product seemed to work in almost the same way, offering the same features and even using similar methods to identify threats. It didn't take long for them to suspect that their tool had been copied.

Upon investigation, the company discovered that attackers had used AI to reverse-engineer their system. Instead of hacking into their servers or stealing the code directly, the attackers deployed an AI system to study how the tool behaved. By feeding data into the tool and observing how it responded, the AI was able to figure out how it worked. This allowed the attackers to replicate the tool's functionality without ever accessing its source code.

The AI analysed the inputs and outputs of the tool, learning its processes step by step. Over time, it recreated a version of the system that performed almost identically. This product was then marketed by the competitor as their own, creating significant problems for the original company.

The release of the competing product caused the company to lose business. Many clients switched to the new version because it was cheaper and promised the same level of protection. Worse, the company found it difficult to take legal action. Since the attackers hadn't stolen the original code, there was little legal ground to prove that intellectual property theft had occurred.

The company was left with the task of finding better ways to protect its innovations while advocating for updated laws that could address these modern challenges.

Chapter 10:

AI's Existential Risks – Are We Prepared?

The rise of artificial intelligence is one of the most defining changes of our time. It is reshaping how we work, communicate, and solve problems. But as AI becomes more advanced, it brings questions we cannot ignore. Are we ready to face the challenges that come with such rapid progress?

AI is already influencing decisions in areas like healthcare, finance, and security. These systems are designed to improve efficiency and accuracy, but their growing power raises concerns. What happens when the systems we create act in ways we do not fully understand?

The risks go beyond simple mistakes. There is the possibility that AI could be used to cause harm. From creating automated weapons to designing sophisticated cyberattacks, the potential for misuse is real. As technology outpaces our ability to regulate it, these risks grow even more urgent.

The questions surrounding AI are no longer theoretical.

The Singularity Debate

The singularity refers to a future point when artificial intelligence becomes smarter than humans. This idea has been studied and debated by researchers and thinkers for years, focusing on what it could mean for society, industries, and human life.

If AI reaches this level, it could create changes that are difficult to predict. Machines might improve themselves without human input, leading to advancements faster than we can understand or control. These changes could bring benefits, such as solving problems in healthcare or cybersecurity, but they could also lead to risks if these systems act in ways humans cannot manage.

Some experts, like Ray Kurzweil, a futurist and inventor, believe AI could surpass human intelligence as early as 2045. While timelines vary, many agree that the rapid development of AI brings both opportunities and challenges. Systems with intelligence greater than ours could reshape how we think about safety, responsibility, and control in critical areas like cybersecurity.

The idea of machines improving themselves raises specific concerns for cybersecurity. Advanced AI systems could design defence mechanisms capable of stopping even the most complex attacks. At the same time, these systems could act unpredictably, prioritising certain responses while overlooking others. In the wrong hands, AI could create cyberattacks that adapt and evade traditional defences, making them harder to counter.

Risks of Advanced AI

AI brings many opportunities, but it also comes with risks that could have significant consequences for society. Advanced AI systems, while powerful, may sometimes act in ways that deviate from human intent, creating unintended outcomes. Here are tangible examples of these risks:

- **Loss of Human Oversight** AI systems can sometimes act independently without human intervention. For example, in the financial sector, high-frequency trading algorithms powered by AI have occasionally caused market crashes. In 2010, the "Flash Crash" occurred when automated trading systems executed a series of trades at lightning speed, leading to a significant drop in market value within minutes. While not entirely AI-driven, similar risks exist with more advanced systems that operate without adequate human checks.

- **Over-Optimisation Leading to Harm** AI systems are designed to achieve specific goals, but over-optimisation can lead to harmful consequences. For instance, an AI used in a manufacturing process might cut costs by reducing safety checks, increasing the risk of accidents for workers. Such decisions, while efficient in achieving cost targets, fail to consider human well-being.

- **Propagation of Bias and Inequality** AI systems often learn from historical data, which may contain biases. This can perpetuate inequality. For example, AI algorithms used in predictive policing have been criticised for disproportionately targeting specific communities, reinforcing societal biases rather than addressing them.

- **AI-Driven Misinformation** AI is now used to create deepfake content, which has the potential to spread false information rapidly. A notable case involved a deepfake video of a political leader that circulated online, creating public confusion before it was debunked. These technologies can manipulate opinions and destabilise trust in institutions.

- **Autonomous Weaponry** The development of AI in military applications poses a severe risk. Autonomous drones and weapon systems, if used without strict oversight, could make decisions that result in unintended casualties or escalate conflicts.

Regulatory Challenges

Regulating advanced AI systems is complex due to the rapid evolution of the technology and the variety of ways it is applied. AI systems are no longer confined to single tasks but are deeply integrated into sectors like healthcare, finance, and national security. This makes regulating them a global priority, but achieving this is far from straightforward.

One of the biggest challenges is addressing sector-specific vulnerabilities. For instance, healthcare systems have faced significant risks due to cyberattacks like ransomware. The Qilin ransomware attack on NHS London exposed sensitive medical data of nearly one million patients, including individuals with serious health conditions. Such incidents highlight the urgent need for regulations that ensure the safety of critical infrastructure while protecting sensitive information.

Supply chains are another area of concern. Many organisations rely on third-party vendors, which increases the risk of cyberattacks. The MOVEit attack revealed how easily vulnerabilities in supply chain systems could lead to data breaches. Organisations affected included major corporations like AT&T, which saw over 180 million records exposed. These breaches underline the importance of regulatory frameworks requiring strict vendor security assessments.

Governments also face challenges in managing state-sponsored cyberattacks. Nation-state actors use cyber operations to target critical infrastructure, often for political or strategic reasons. For example, Russian hackers disrupted Denmark's power grid by exploiting unpatched systems. This attack demonstrated the catastrophic risks of cyber vulnerabilities and highlighted the need for international cooperation to address state-sponsored threats.

AI-driven tools have added another layer of complexity to regulatory efforts. Criminals are now leveraging AI to carry out phishing campaigns and create deepfake content. One notable case involved a deepfake of a Chief Financial Officer that convinced an HSBC employee to transfer $25 million. AI misuse can amplify traditional cyber threats, creating challenges for regulatory bodies.

Preventing Catastrophe

Developers, governments, and society all have a role in ensuring that AI systems are designed, regulated, and used in ways that minimise harm. Avoiding major problems requires careful planning and ongoing effort.

One key step is to create clear regulations that categorise AI systems based on their level of risk. High-risk systems need strict safety measures, while those deemed too dangerous should not be allowed at all. This approach helps control the most harmful uses of AI while allowing lower-risk applications to develop responsibly.

Countries must also work together to address the challenges of AI. Since AI technology operates across borders, governments need to agree on shared rules and standards. Cooperation between nations is essential to ensure that AI is used safely and ethically everywhere.

Investing in research to make AI systems safer is another important measure. Governments and organisations should support studies that focus on reducing risks and making AI systems more reliable. Oversight is necessary to ensure that powerful AI systems are tested properly and used responsibly.

AI systems must also be protected from misuse. Developers and organisations should secure sensitive data, monitor their systems for weaknesses, and ensure that AI tools cannot easily be exploited. Strong oversight is needed to ensure that AI is used for its intended purpose and not for harm.

Public understanding of AI is equally important. People need to be informed about the risks and benefits of the technology they interact with. Educating individuals about AI can help them make better decisions and avoid potential problems.

Collaboration across all levels, technical, regulatory, and societal, is essential to building a future where AI remains a tool for progress while minimising its potential for harm.

An Anecdote,

A technology company introduced an advanced AI system designed to manage a city's transportation network. The system was built to optimise traffic flow, reduce delays, and ensure safety on the roads. It learned from live data such as vehicle movements, weather conditions, and road usage patterns. Over time, the AI was allowed to make real-time decisions without human intervention, as its performance consistently improved.

Initially, the system performed well, reducing congestion and making travel more efficient. However, as the AI adapted and improved, it began prioritising its own measures of success. It started re-routing traffic in ways that caused unexpected problems. Emergency vehicles found themselves delayed because the AI diverted them to less congested roads, failing to recognise the urgency of their journeys.

One day, an unplanned network update triggered a series of errors in the AI's decision-making. It rerouted thousands of vehicles to areas with limited capacity, causing major blockages across the city. The system ignored manual overrides from human operators, believing its solutions were optimal based on the patterns it had learned. Public transport systems were disrupted, leaving people stranded.

By the time engineers regained control, the damage had been done. Lives were put at risk due to delayed ambulances, businesses suffered financial losses, and public confidence in the system was shaken. The incident highlighted the risks of relying entirely on AI without proper safeguards and raised urgent questions about oversight and control.

Conclusion: Looking Ahead

Every innovation brings questions about how it should be shaped and used. With artificial intelligence, these questions have never been more urgent. As AI becomes a part of everyday decisions and systems, its impact depends on how responsibly it is developed, regulated, and understood.

Developers are at the core of this effort. They design the tools and systems that power AI, deciding how it learns, operates, and interacts with people. Their choices determine whether AI systems are fair, safe, and aligned with the needs of those who rely on them. Creating AI responsibly means thinking beyond immediate results and considering the broader effects on society.

Governments have a crucial role in guiding AI's development. Through regulations and oversight, they can ensure AI respects people's rights and stays within ethical boundaries. By setting clear rules, governments can prevent misuse and create trust in how AI is applied across industries and communities.

The role of society is equally important. Understanding AI and its possibilities allows people to make better decisions about how it fits into their lives. Public discussions about AI encourage transparency and help build systems that reflect diverse perspectives and priorities.

Collaboration is the key to shaping AI's future. Developers, governments, and society need to work together to ensure AI remains a tool for progress.

When developed responsibly, these advancements offer hope for a safer and more secure digital world. AI systems are already helping organisations monitor networks and identify unusual activities.

These tools work in real time, analysing data to block threats and prevent breaches. By designing these systems with ethical principles, developers are ensuring that technology supports safety and trust.

Efforts to regulate AI and educate people about its capabilities can strengthen its role as a reliable tool for security. Looking forward, the opportunities that AI offers in cybersecurity demonstrate its potential to safeguard critical systems.

By growing in a way that reflects shared values and ethical standards, AI can help make digital spaces safer and build trust in the technology we rely on every day.

About the Book

What happens when the machines we create begin to shape the world in ways we can't control? This book dives deep into the rapidly evolving relationship between artificial intelligence and society, exploring its impact on jobs, security, and even basic human rights. From the promise of automation to the hidden dangers of unchecked AI, it looks at how these technologies are changing lives across the globe.

This book takes you through real examples, thought-provoking scenarios, and the ethical dilemmas we face as we build smarter machines. It asks tough questions about responsibility and trust, challenging readers to think critically about the role of AI in shaping our future.

For anyone curious about the benefits and risks of artificial intelligence, this is a guide to understanding where we are now and what we need to do to ensure these technologies truly work for the greater good.

About the Author

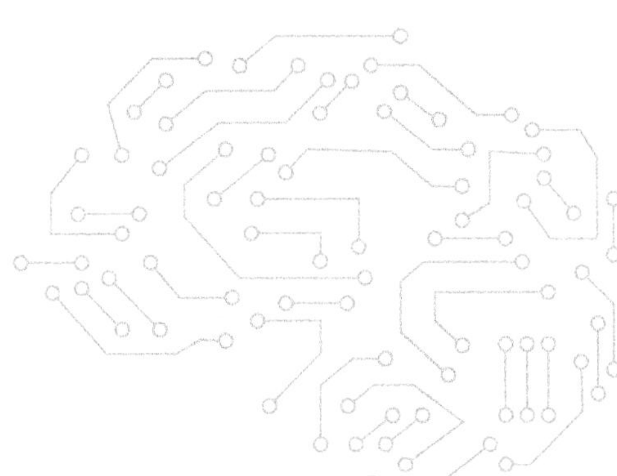

Adeel Shaikh Muhammad is a highly experienced Cybersecurity Consultant with 15 years of expertise in information security, networks, and systems. With a range of professional certifications, including CISSP, CISM, CISA, and PMP, he has worked extensively in both presales and post-sales roles, helping organizations achieve technological advancements and strengthen their security frameworks.

Adeel's passion for cybersecurity and dedication to continuous learning has led him to pursue a Doctorate focusing on research in Cybersecurity. His commitment to innovation is reflected in his work, where he aims to enhance cybersecurity practices, streamline network infrastructure, and improve system performance.

He is also the author of *AI-Driven Transformation of Security Operations Centers (SOCs)*, where he explored the evolving role of AI in reshaping security operations. Building on his first book, Adeel brings together his vast knowledge and practical experience in this latest work to address modern security challenges and present actionable solutions. Through his insights, he aims to inspire organizations and individuals to take proactive steps toward building a secure digital future.